21st Century Skills Library

COOL SCIENCE CAREERS

NANOTECHNOLOGIST

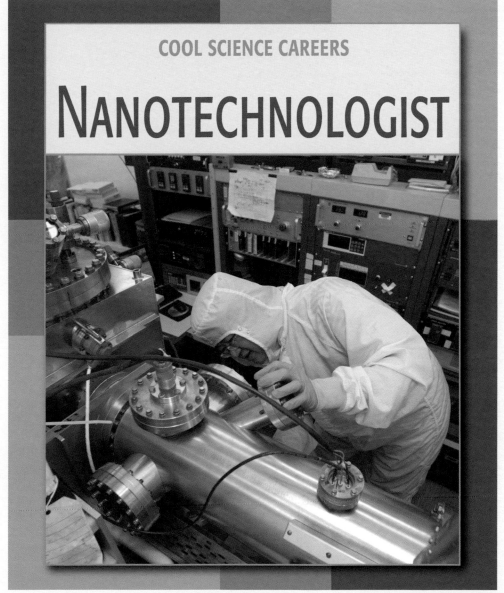

Ann Heinrichs

Cherry Lake Publishing
Ann Arbor, Michigan

Published in the United States of America by Cherry Lake Publishing
Ann Arbor, Michigan
www.cherrylakepublishing.com

Content Advisers: Rashid Bashir, PhD, Director, Micro and Nanotechnology Laboratory,
University of Illinois, and Irfan Ahmad, PhD, Associate Director, Center for Nanoscale
Science and Technology, University of Illionis

Photo Credits: Cover and pages 1, 11, and 17, Photo courtesy of University of Illinois
Center for Nanoscale Science and Technology, Micro and Nanotechnology Laboratory,
Urbana, Illinois, 2008; page 4, ©Phil Wigglesworth/Alamy; page 6, ©Mary Evans Picture
Library/Alamy; page 12 and 20, ©vario images GmbH & Co.KG/Alamy; page 14, ©Henry
Westheim Photography/Alamy; page 19, ©iStockphoto.com/mrloz; page 23, ©Fotocrisis,
used under license from Shutterstock, Inc.; page 24, ©AP Photo/Eckehard Schulz

Library of Congress Cataloging-in-Publication Data
Heinrichs, Ann.
 Nanotechnologist / by Ann Heinrichs.
    p. cm.—(Cool science careers)
 Includes index.
 ISBN-13: 978-1-60279-307-1
 ISBN-10: 1-60279-307-7
 1. Nanotechnologists—Juvenile literature. 2. Nanotechnology—Juvenile
 literature. I. Title.
 T174.7.H44 2008
 620'.5—dc22   2008029288

Cherry Lake Publishing would like to acknowledge the work of
The Partnership for 21st Century Skills.
Please visit www.21stcenturyskills.org *for more information.*

TABLE OF CONTENTS

CHAPTER ONE

THINK SMALL

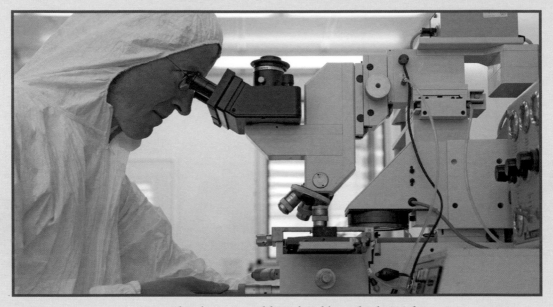

*Nanotechnologists would not be able to do their jobs
without the help of very powerful microscopes.*

Have you ever built things with Lego blocks? In a way, that's what nanotechnologists do. Except that their "blocks" are tiny particles a million times smaller than the period at the end of this sentence. Using a special microscope, they move those particles around. They build them into new shapes, such as towers, tubes, or balls. Those new structures are materials that can do amazing things.

Take a look at nanotechnologist Graciela Padua. She works with zein, a substance found in corn. By rebuilding zein, she produced a kind of artificial skin. For people with serious burns or wounds, it can help their skin grow back and heal. Dr. Padua invents fun things with zein, too. She developed a kind of chewing gum that won't stick to the bottom of your shoes!

Nanotechnologists work with very tiny things. They need to measure those things in nanometers. The **prefix** *nano-* comes from the Greek word for "dwarf." When used with a unit of measure, *nano-* means "one-billionth." How big is a nanometer? Well, let's start with meters first.

One meter is about 39 inches, or 3 feet plus 3 inches. That's about as high as a newborn baby elephant. A meter is made up of 100 centimeters. One centimeter is about as long as a ladybug. Each centimeter consists of 10 millimeters. One millimeter is about the size of a large grain of sand. And each millimeter contains 1 million nanometers. Going back to that meter, it consists of 1 billion nanometers. In other words, 1 nanometer is one-billionth of a meter. Take a look at one of your hairs. It's about 80,000 nanometers thick!

Nanotechnologists work with things from 1 to 100 nanometers in size. This is called working at the nanoscale. They move things around and build things, just as you might move pieces on a checkerboard or build a birdhouse. But instead of using checkers or wood, they use molecules.

Molecules are tiny particles of matter. One molecule of water is the smallest unit of water that exists. Just one drop of water contains more than 1 quintillion water molecules. That's the same as 1 billion billion molecules, or 1,000,000,000,000,000,000! Nanotechnologists work with even smaller particles called atoms. They are the particles that molecules are made of. That water molecule, for

Richard Feynman was awarded the Nobel Prize in physics in 1965.

example, is built out of two hydrogen atoms and one oxygen atom.

Nanotechnologists watch how molecules and atoms behave. But they can do much more than watch. They can control and change the way those particles behave. They can push atoms around and even design new molecules. This produces new materials that are stronger, lighter, cheaper, and more useful.

People first began to think about nanotechnology in 1959. That's when **physicist** Richard Feynman gave a speech titled "There's Plenty of Room at the Bottom."

Feynman said it should be possible to move things "atom by atom." Take "all the information . . . in all the books in the world," he said. You could store that information in a space as small as a tiny speck of dust.

The scanning tunneling microscope was invented in 1981. It enabled scientists to observe atoms up close for the first time. They soon discovered that atoms and molecules at the nanoscale behave differently from how they do in big quantities. They saw they could put these particles together in different ways to produce amazing new materials.

In 1985, scientists discovered fullerenes. These are clusters of **carbon** atoms arranged in unusual ways. That led to the discovery of tunnel-shaped carbon molecules called carbon nanotubes. They are 100 times stronger than steel but weigh much less. Soon products using nanotubes began appearing.

K. Eric Drexler took nanotechnology to an exciting new level. He believed people could build molecules into tiny machines. These machines could manufacture objects such as computers or medical devices in great quantities with incredible speed. Such products could be "as low-cost as potatoes." Drexler called this process molecular manufacturing. He explained his ideas in his 1986 book *Engines of Creation*.

So far, no one has found a way to make molecular manufacturing work. Some scientists are not sure if it's possible. Others are uncertain of how soon the scientific processes can be developed. Still, many scientists find

Nanotechnologists James Tour and Kevin Kelly designed a nanocar in 2005. It was made of just one molecule. Its "wheels" were fullerenes—60-atom balls of carbon—attached to each of the four corners. Tour and Kelly wanted to find out how fullerenes move along a metal surface. Would the fullerenes roll like real wheels? Or would they just slip and slide? If a molecule could be made to roll, it would be a big step toward performing tasks at the nanoscale. It took Tour and Kelly almost 8 years to make the nanocar work. The hardest part was figuring out how to attach the wheels without destroying the rest of the car. As it turned out, at a high temperature the fullerenes rotated instead of sliding. The car rolled!

Learning & Innovation Skills

Eric Drexler saw that plants and animals have machines working inside them. These machines are complex molecules. They do tasks such as turning food into energy and making muscles move. Drexler believed people could build nanomachines that worked the same way. He also imagined that nanomachines would be able to make copies of themselves, just as plants and animals reproduce. Do you think this is possible? Why or why not?

the idea of molecular manufacturing exciting. They are looking for ways it could be used to make new medicines and other helpful materials.

Every day, nanotechnologists are solving problems, developing new materials, and helping people live better lives. If you were a nanotechnologist, you might discover a cure for cancer. You might find a way to heal blindness or heart disease. You might invent a spacecraft that travels faster than the speed of light. Or a computer the size of a pinpoint. Who knows? Maybe you'll be the first to build a molecule-sized factory!

CHAPTER TWO

WORKING AT THE NANOSCALE

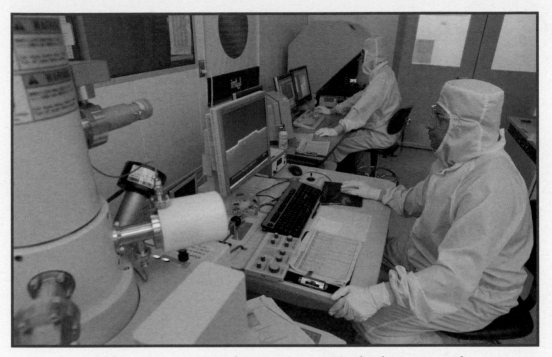

A student uses a scanning electron microscope in the clean room at the Micro and Nanotechnology Laboratory at the University of Illinois.

Suppose you were looking for a nanotechnologist. Would you look up "nanotechnologist" in the phone book's Yellow Pages? If you did, you wouldn't find such a listing. That's because nanotechnologists don't work in a science all their own. Instead, they work within many areas of study.

A scientist does research at the Institute for New Materials, in Saarbrücken, Germany. Nanotechnology research labs are full of high-tech equipment.

Some nanotechnologists work in chemistry, physics, engineering, computer science, or materials science. Some work in biological sciences or medicine. Others work in agriculture, food science, or environmental science.

If you were a nanotechnologist, your workspace would be a **research lab**. That lab might be in a university or a large medical center. It might be in a private company. The U.S. government has nanotechnology research centers, too. They are located in universities around the country. Their scientists study everything from metals and light waves to the environment and disease control.

As a nanotechnologist, your first problem would be finding a way to see extremely tiny things—things as small as an atom. You would solve that problem by using special microscopes. The basic tool for many nanotechnologists is a scanning probe microscope (SPM). Two commonly used SPMs are scanning tunneling microscopes and atomic force microscopes.

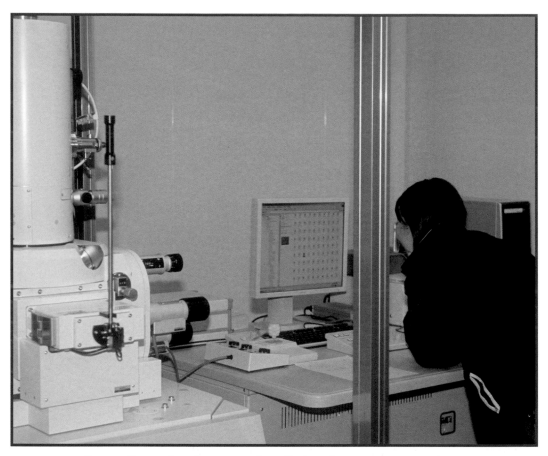

Images from microscopes are often displayed on computer monitors.
This makes it easier for researchers to study them.

Each of these microscopes has a tiny tip that runs over
a material and detects atom-sized details. An image of
these details appears on a large screen. The tip can also
be used to poke or nudge atoms and molecules into new
patterns. Biologists use SPMs to look inside human cells.

They might figure out how to "teach" a cell not to pick up a disease. Computer scientists use SPMs to look inside a computer **microchip**. They can use it to design smaller, faster microchips.

In a nanotechnology lab, you'll see huge machines connected by lots of wires. Some machines sit on a tabletop. Others almost reach the ceiling. You may see large metal tanks or tubes and glass-covered cases. Monitors, or computer screens, show lists, numbers, and colorful patterns. What are all these machines? One is probably a scanning probe microscope. Another might be a spinner. It spins around to coat a surface evenly with a new test material. You might see an evaporator. It uses a vacuum to pump water out of a material or to create a completely clean space. Other machines could be ovens, rinsers, or dryers.

Some nanotechnology research takes place in a clean room. That's a sealed room with very low levels of dust, germs, and other particles. These particles can **pollute** the materials scientists are working on. Clean-room workers wear protective suits, face masks, gloves, and boots. These outfits protect the workers from the materials. They also protect the materials from the workers.

Outside of a clean room, many nanotechnologists wear white lab coats and protective gloves. Others wear their ordinary, everyday clothes when they're working. Who knows what they will wear in the future. Nanotechnologists have already developed some exciting new clothing fibers and materials. They can change colors or even stop bullets!

CHAPTER THREE

BECOMING A NANOTECHNOLOGIST

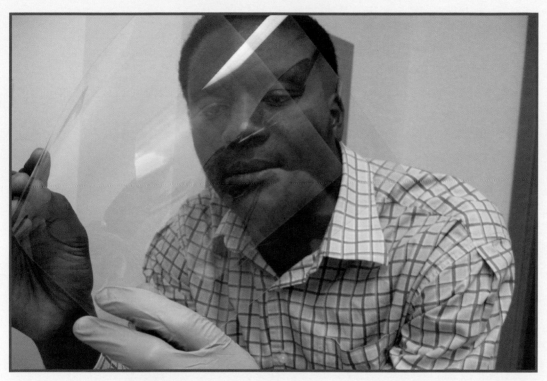

A graduate student examines special sensors at the University of Illinois Micro and Nanotechnology Laboratory in 2007.

Are you curious about the world around you? Do you find yourself wondering why and how things work the way they do? Do you fiddle around with things and try to make them work better? If so, nanotechnology could be the career for you.

It's fun to see what real nanotechnologists were like as kids. Here are some of their stories:

One liked working puzzles and building with Lego blocks. Now she builds molecules into materials that can be used in space exploration. One was fascinated with wildlife. He was always bringing stray or injured animals home. Now he studies nanotubes in tiny water creatures. One loved making things with modeling clay. Now he builds molecules that can detect life in materials from other planets. Many nanotechnologists had science projects at home when they were kids. They collected leaves, memorized the planets, took clocks apart, or launched toy rockets.

If you'd like to become a nanotechnologist, you can begin preparing now, even before high school. Math and science are important subjects for future scientists. Visiting science museums is a fun way to learn about science, too.

Taking science classes is a great way to help you decide if you might enjoy a career as a nanotechnologist.

You might even be able to check out labs and science centers in your area. Many of them offer tours and other educational programs for middle-school students.

In high school, you can take math, biology, chemistry, and physics classes. Computer skills are valuable, too. All nanotechnologists rely on computers in their jobs. Some nanotechnology labs accept high school students

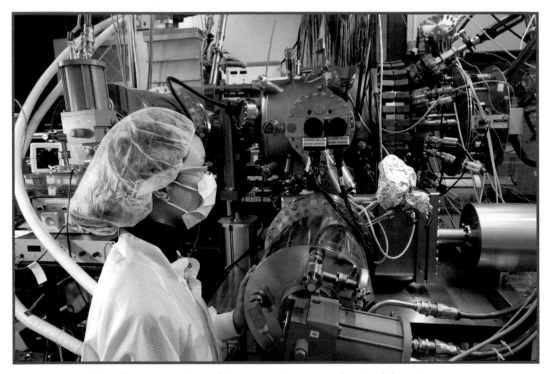

*Hands-on experience doing experiments and using lab equipment
is a crucial part of a nanotechnologist's education.*

as summer **interns**. As an intern, you work alongside
nanotechnologists and help them on their projects.

At some point, you will realize which field of science
excites you the most. It may be biology, chemistry, physics,
engineering, or computer science. You may be interested in
medicine, space, or the environment. This will guide you
in choosing a major subject for college. No matter what

your major is, you need to have good work and study habits. As one nanotechnologist says, "Being a patient and creative problem solver is really important."

After college, most nanotechnologists enter university programs to earn doctoral degrees. Then they spend lots of time in the lab. They learn research methods and do **experiments** that no one has ever tried before. Often they are part of a team of scientists working on a project together. They may teach younger students, too.

After getting a doctorate, a nanotechnologist may go to work in a university. He or she may combine teaching and research. Some nanotechnologists

If you're interested in nanotechnology, you should choose a college or university with strong programs in your special interest areas. A parent, teacher, school counselor, or scientist friend can help with this decision. It is important to figure where your learning needs will best be met. Then it's important to perform well in your chosen subjects.

join research groups in government labs or private companies. Others take more science courses. Even at this point, it's not unusual to change areas of research. After working in biochemistry, for example, someone may switch to food science.

In a way, a nanotechnologist's education is never complete. There's always more to learn. New developments in the nanosciences are happening every day. They promise an endless array of new problems to solve and new discoveries to be made.

CHAPTER FOUR

A BOLD, NEW FUTURE

Scientists hope to develop nanorobots and other tiny devices that would be able to destroy human cancer cells without harming healthy ones.

A man is infected with nanorobots. They work inside his body, changing how he looks, thinks, and feels. He must find out why this is happening! So goes the plot of a 1980s novel.

Nanotechnology was once the stuff of science fiction. In just a short time, it has become science fact. Now it's one of the most exciting and fastest-growing sciences in the world.

Scientists have reproduced the self-cleaning properties of lotus leaves in the roofing tile on the left.

Scientists today believe nanorobots are a real possibility. These molecule-sized nanomachines would contain motors and computers. Their tiny robot arms could reach out and grab things. And they could be trained to perform specific tasks.

Researchers in nanomedicine are especially interested in nanorobots. An army of nanorobots could invade a sick person. They could battle whatever is causing the disease and destroy it. This would be faster, cheaper, and more effective than present-day treatments.

Another promising area for nanotechnology is the environment. Nanofilters could clean our air and water. Newly developed nanomaterials could check for pollution in the environment. Dangerous substances could be detected and removed before they harm anyone.

Nanotechnologists are also working on new sources of energy that don't pollute the air. For example, they are developing new kinds of solar cells. Solar cells take in energy from the sun's rays. They change that energy into heat and light. Nanoscale solar cells could be produced cheaply and in great quantities. With enough of them, we could stop burning coal, oil, and

Many nanotechnologists get their ideas from processes in the natural world. For example, researchers are studying the leaves of the lotus, an Asian water lily. When rain falls on the lotus, very little water actually touches the leaf. In part, nanohairs on the leaf keep the water off the surface. When the water drop rolls off, it collects dirt along the way. Scientists hope to apply this process in developing self-cleaning windows, fabrics, and other materials. Can you think of any other applications that nanotechnologists might develop by studying the nanohairs on lotus leaves?

other fuels. This would improve the environment and the climate worldwide.

Some nanotechnologists hope to eliminate animal testing. New drugs, cosmetics, and foods must be tested before they're approved for human use. Those tests are often done on animals. Nanotechnology can offer other ways to test a new product. One idea is to test a nanoscale amount of the substance on human cells in the lab.

The nanomachines of the future might be able to build other nanomachines. They would work like factories, churning out tiny machines with dazzling speed. So far, scientists have managed to make some very simple molecular machines. With more research, though, molecular manufacturing has a bright future.

When Eric Drexler introduced the idea of molecular manufacturing, he included a warning. His nanorobots would be able to duplicate themselves. One mistake or accident, and they might grow out of control. They could swell into a "grey goo" that gobbles up the world. Now Drexler says he's sorry he ever used the term *grey goo*. People who oppose or fear nanotechnology like to bring up scary scenes of the grey goo.

The grey goo **scenario** is not likely to happen. Even Drexler says so. Still, nanotechnology may have dangers we can't predict. Nanoscale molecules behave in ways completely different from those of larger particles. They may be safe in a larger form but unsafe or even poisonous in nanoscale sizes. Suppose nanoparticles were released into the

21st Century Content

Berkeley, California, became the nation's first city to pass a public health law regulating nanotechnology. The city is home to the University of California's Lawrence Berkeley National Laboratory. It's one of the top nanotechnology research centers in the country. In 2006, the Berkeley City Council voted to classify nanoparticles as hazardous materials. This requires the city's researchers to report on their nanotechnology materials and how they are handling them. Do you think this will help or hurt nanotechnology research? Why?

air and waterways. Scientists and ordinary citizens are concerned about the health problems this could cause.

In spite of possible hazards, nanotechnology is here to stay. The benefits are just too attractive. Using nanotechnology, scientists could build tiny, super-fast computers that cost less than a penny. They could find new ways to make dirty water clean enough to drink. They might build tiny machines that make repairs inside the body. And they could develop cheaper ways to grow food plants. Nanotechnologists love the work they do. They are finding ways to improve human life around the world.

Some Famous Nanotechnologists

Ilesanmi Adesida (1949–) has received worldwide recognition for his research and innovative techniques. He has worked on nanoscale materials processing and developed high-speed microelectronic devices and circuits. His discoveries have been used in computers, cell phones, and other electronic equipment.

Gerd Binning (1947–) and **Heinrich Rohrer (1933–)** invented the scanning tunneling microscope in 1981. The STM was the first microscope that enabled scientists to observe individual atoms closely. The two won the 1986 Nobel Prize in physics for their invention.

K. Eric Drexler (1955–) is often called the father of nanotechnology. In his 1986 book *Engines of Creation,* he introduced the idea of molecular manufacturing. In 1991, Drexler became the first person to receive a PhD in molecular nanotechnology.

Don Eigler (1954?–) is a physicist. In 1989, he used a scanning tunneling microscope to spell out the letters *IBM* with atoms. This proved for the first time that individual atoms could be moved in a precise way.

Richard Feynman (1918–1988) was a physicist. He is best known for his speech titled "There's Plenty of Room at the Bottom." In this 1959 talk, he introduced the idea of moving one atom at a time to build things at the nanoscale.

Chad Mirkin (1963–) is a professor of chemistry, medicine, biomedical engineering, biological and chemical engineering, and materials science and engineering at Northwestern University. He holds more than 300 patents and is considered one of the world's top nanotechnology researchers.

John Rogers (1967–) has won many awards for his work. He is a leader in the development of flexible nanoscale electronic components. These innovative "soft" materials will lead to the development of better artificial limbs and other medical devices as well as better machine parts.

Richard Smalley (1943–2005) was a chemist and physicist. In 1985, he and his research associates discovered clusters of carbon atoms called fullerenes. They received the 1996 Nobel Prize in chemistry for this discovery.

Glossary

carbon (KAR-buhn) a chemical element present in all life-forms; one of the many chemical elements

cells (SELZ) tiny building blocks that all animals and plants are composed of

experiments (ek-SPER-uh-ments) scientific tests to try out an idea or see what happens under certain conditions

interns (IN-turnz) people who assist professionals or train with them in order to gain experience

lab (LAB) a place with the equipment and conditions for doing scientific studies; short for "laboratory"

microchip (MYE-kroh-chip) a tiny electrical device that makes computers, cell phones, and many other products work

microscope (MYE-kruh-skope) an instrument that gives a close-up view of very small objects

physicist (FIZZ-uh-sist) a scientist who studies matter, motion, and energy

pollute (puh-LOOT) to make something unclean by introducing a harmful substance

prefix (PREE-fiks) a set of letters added at the beginning of a word

research (REE-surch) detailed scientific study to find out information about something

scenario (suh-NAIR-ree-oh) outline of a set of events that might happen in a particular situation

For More Information

Books

Bourne, Marlene. *MEMS & Nanotechnology for Kids.*
Scottsdale, AZ: Bourne Research LLC, 2007.

Harmer, J. Andrea. *Nanotechnology for Grades 1–6+: Introducing
Nan and Bucky Dog.* Bloomington, IN: AuthorHouse, 2005.

Jefferis, David. *Micro Machines: Ultra-Small World of
Nanotechnology.* New York: Crabtree, 2006.

Johnson, Rebecca L. *Nanotechnology.* Minneapolis: Lerner Publications, 2006.

Maddox, Dianne. *Nanotechnology: Science on the Edge.*
Farmington Hills, MI: Blackbirch Press, 2005.

Web Sites

Nanooze!
www.nanooze.org
Check out the latest nanotechnology news, post on the Nanooze!
blog, and learn more about leading nanotechnologists

The Nanozone
www.nanozone.org
Learn more about nanotechnology and the scientists who work on it

INDEX

ABOUT THE AUTHOR

Ann Heinrichs is the author of more than 200 books for children and young adults. They cover U.S. and world history and culture, science and nature, and English grammar. Ann has also enjoyed careers as a children's book editor and an advertising copywriter. An avid traveler, she has toured Europe, Africa, the Middle East, and East Asia. Born in Fort Smith, Arkansas, she now lives in Chicago. She enjoys biking, kayaking, and flying kites.